PLANET POWER

Explore the World's Renewable Energy

written by Stacy P. Clark

illustrated by Annalisa Beghelli

Barefoot Books
step inside a story

Imagine blue skies and golden sun,
Where the wind blows and rivers run:
Our precious world of land and sea,
Harnessing mighty energy.

Electricity is a type of **energy** that can be used to power trains, machines and lights.

Hydropower

The flowing water in **rivers** can be used to make electricity.

When the rain falls,
Water flows
Through creeks and streams —
Off it goes.

When the rain falls,
Rivers tumble.
From wondrous peaks,
Waterfalls rumble.

Hydropower

A **turbine** is a machine that spins when water, steam or wind passes through it. The spinning of the turbine powers a generator that gives us electricity.

When the rain falls,
Water power
Flows through dams
Every hour.

When the rain falls,
Turbines roar.
Clean energy powers
Mills onshore.

Solar Power

When the sun shines,
Rooftops gleam.
Solar panels
Catch sunbeams.

A **solar panel** turns light from the sun into electricity.

When the sun shines,
Inside each panel,
Renewable power
Flows through a channel.

Solar Power

When the sun shines
On open spaces,
Big solar farms
Power lively places.

A large area covered with solar panels is called a **solar farm**.

When the sun shines,
Golden rays
Fuel electric cars
And speedy railways.

Wind Power

When the wind blows,
Giant blades swirl.
Gears rotate,
Magnets whirl.

When the wind blows,
Energy surges.
Through power lines
It flows and merges.

When the wind blows through a turbine, the wind's energy makes the **blades** turn.

When the wind blows,
Landscapes change.
New wind farms stretch
Across the range.

A **wind farm** is a group of wind turbines in the same location.

When the wind blows,
Cities hustle.
Sky trains glide.
People bustle.

Tidal Power

When the tides shift,
The minnows run,
Darting to and fro
Below the setting sun.

The water level of the ocean rises and falls every day. These patterns are called **tides**.

When the tides shift,
Seas fall and rise.
Tidal rivers move
From lows to highs.

Tidal Power

When the tides shift,
Turbines spin
As currents rush out
And then back in.

When the tides shift,
Clean energy
Powers sparkling cities
By the sea.

Clean energy can be turned into electricity to power trains, machines and lights while also protecting the water, air and land.

NY 875

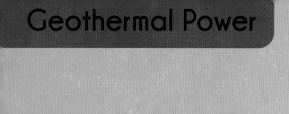

When the heat rises
From Earth's deep zones,
It travels up
Through rocks and stones.

In some areas of the world, the Earth has **heat** trapped in rocks beneath the surface.

When the heat rises,
Steam zips through pipes,
Across green valleys,
Past zebra stripes.

Geothermal Power

Steam is formed when water boils and can be used to spin turbines.

When the heat rises,
Workers cheer.
The steam drives turbines
Through the year.

When the heat rises,
Geothermal sites
Power lowland towns
And hillside heights.

When the waves roll,
Surfers glide.
On glossy boards
They catch a ride.

A **buoy** is an object that floats on ocean waves. Some buoys capture energy from the movement of the waves to make electricity.

When the waves roll,
A buoy dips.
Energy flows,
Power rips.

Wave Power

Since **waves** are found all over the world's oceans, they can supply electricity to any place near the coast.

When the waves roll
Towards the shore,
They power seaside shops,
Cable cars and more.

When the waves roll,
Waterfront lights
Shine like diamonds
In the night.

Rushing rivers, oceans and tides
Make clean energy to power our lives.
The sun, Earth's heat and breezes too
Help our planet stay green and blue.

Why Do We Need Renewable Energy?

In countries all around the world, people rely on **electricity** to power their lives. We use electricity for everything from lighting buildings in giant cities to pumping water for drinking in rural areas.

For well over 100 years, coal, oil and natural gas, otherwise known as **fossil fuels**, have been the main source of the world's electricity. Fossil fuels are made from the broken-down remains of plants and animals, found deep below the ground. When fossil fuels are used, they cannot be replaced. They are a limited resource.

Scientists have learned that using fossil fuels harms our planet. When they are burned, they release **carbon dioxide**, a gas that traps the sun's heat close to Earth. This makes the planet warmer overall.

As the world has heated up, weather and water cycles have changed. This is called **climate change**. Droughts, forest fires, flooding and hurricanes have become more common all over the globe. As glaciers and ice caps melt faster, sea levels are rising along coastlines where people live. These types of changes in our climate are dangerous for people, plants and animals.

Explore Renewable Energy Around the World

Renewable energy is an important part of how we help to reduce climate change. Renewable energy comes from Earth's **natural resources**, including water, sunshine, wind and heat. These resources are replaced, or renewed, every time they are used, so they'll never run out.

More importantly, renewable energy does less damage to the planet's water, land and air, also known as the environment. It does not release carbon dioxide into the air like fossil fuels do. Renewable energy is sometimes called **clean energy**. It is kinder to our planet than "dirty" fossil fuels, which change the environment making it harder for people, animals and plants to survive.

The map below highlights where you can find the six renewable energy projects shown in this book. But each type of technology can be found in many other places around the world!

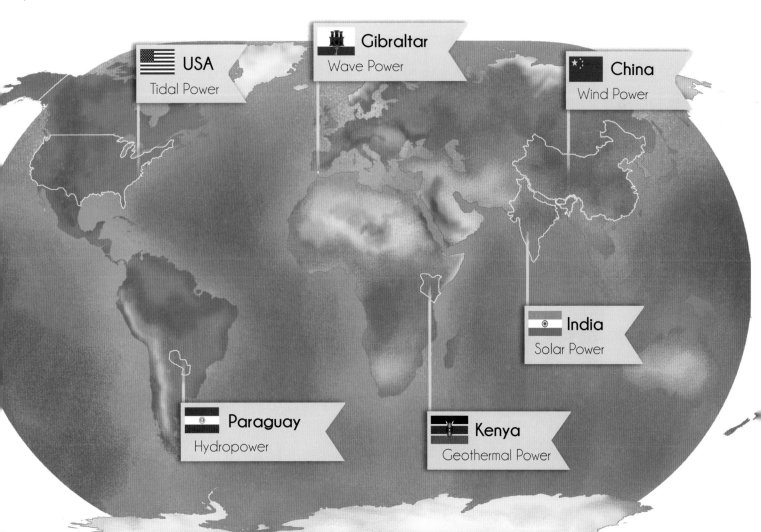

USA — Tidal Power

Gibraltar — Wave Power

China — Wind Power

India — Solar Power

Paraguay — Hydropower

Kenya — Geothermal Power

How Does it Work?

Most ways of producing electricity involve spinning a **turbine**, which looks like a fast-moving wheel. The turbine's rotation (spinning) powers an electrical **generator** made of magnets and copper wire, which produces electricity.

When fossil fuels are burned, the heat created is used to boil water, which produces steam, which makes turbines spin. For renewable energy, we use other resources to make the turbines spin — this can be the wind, the tides, rushing rivers, rolling waves or the rising heat from beneath Earth's surface.

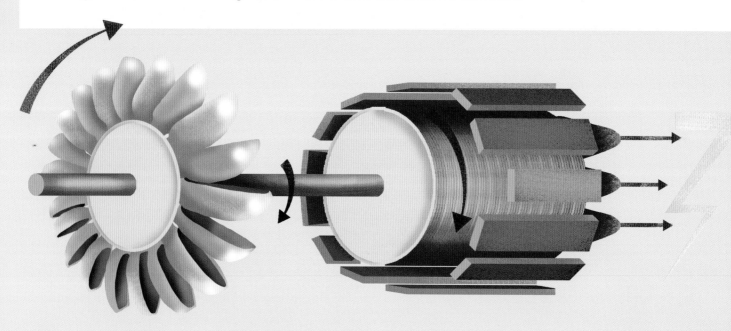

A **turbine** is a machine that spins to power a generator, which makes electricity.

A **generator** is made of magnets and copper wire, which spin together to form an electrical current.

When a turbine spins a generator, the magnets and copper wire spin together quickly. This motion makes **electrons** (tiny, charged particles in the wire) move. This movement of electrons through the wire is the electric current that we call electricity.

Electricity can power machines, turn on lights, warm and cool buildings and charge electric cars, trains, buses, trucks and scooters! We share electricity with people living in different areas by building electrical transmission lines, also called power lines.

Hydropower

Moving water can be used to generate electricity. When rivers rush through **dams**, their energy is captured as hydropower.

River dams create man-made lakes, called **reservoirs**. When water is released from these reservoirs, it rushes through the dam's **hydroturbines**, making them spin.

Paraguay, a country in the middle of South America, is known for its many mighty rivers. The Itaipú Dam at 200 m (650 ft) tall is one of the world's largest hydropower projects. The dam reaches across the Paraná River on the border of Paraguay and Brazil, so these countries share the electricity that the dam's water produces.

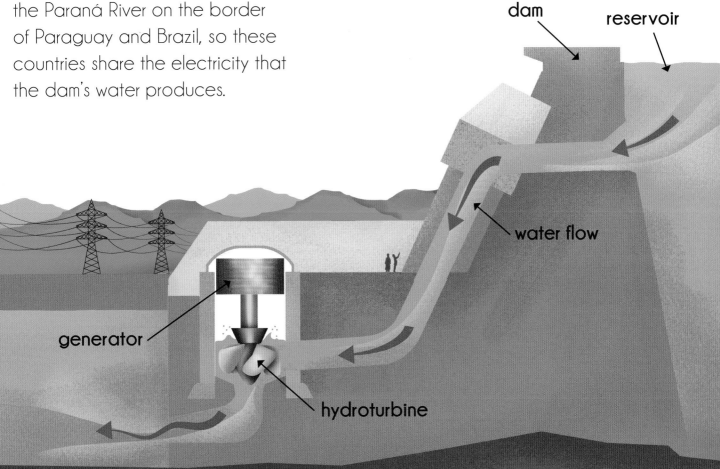

dam

reservoir

water flow

generator

hydroturbine

Solar Power

Solar power harnesses the energy in the sun's rays to produce electricity. Unlike many other forms of renewable energy, solar power does not use turbines.

Solar panels are made of thin layers of a shiny material called silicon. Silicon easily carries electrical current. When sunlight falls onto the layers of silicon, electrons flow out of the panel into a wire, making electricity. The **inverter** allows this electricity to be used in homes. The **meter** measures how much electricity has been made.

You can find solar panels on rooftops or on the ground. A solar farm is created when many panels are fitted into platforms on the ground, known as solar arrays.

In **India**, where the sun shines about 300 days a year, solar-powered rooftops and solar farms generate renewable electricity. Pavagada, in southern India, is one of the country's largest solar farms, covering an area the size of 10,000 football fields!

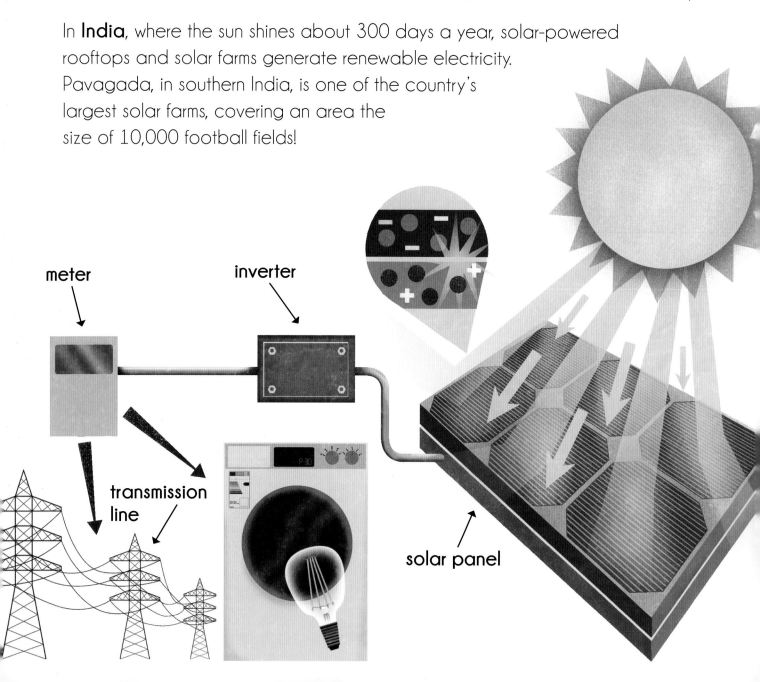

meter

inverter

transmission
line

solar panel

Wind Power

The strength of the wind can be captured by wind turbines to make electricity.

Wind turbines have three giant turbine **blades** connected by a central **hub**. The blades and the hub together are called the rotor. Each blade is shaped like a plane wing. When the wind blows, the rotor spins and turns the **gears**. The spinning gears provide the speed needed to power a **generator**, which

in turn makes electricity. Some of the largest wind turbines in the world are almost as tall as the Eiffel Tower!

Wind turbines are often grouped together into wind farms either on land or out at sea. Land-based wind farms all over northern **China** send electricity from rural areas to the busy, large cities in the east. At a length of 3,400 km (2,100 miles), the Changji-Guquan electrical transmission line is the largest and longest project of its kind.

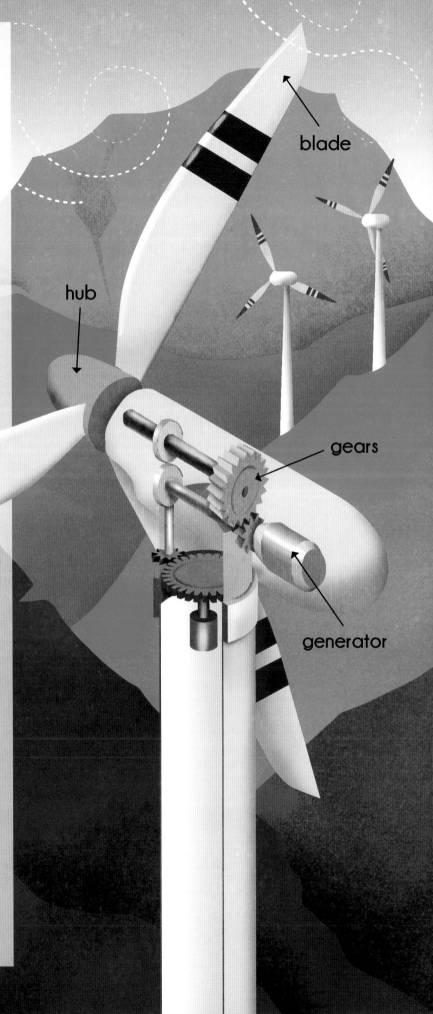

blade

hub

gears

generator

Tidal Power

The rise and fall of ocean and sea tides can be used to generate electricity using **tidal turbines**.

Tidal turbines look a bit like the propellers of a plane. Mounted onto a **frame**, the turbines are lowered onto the floor of the ocean in an area with strong tides. The movement of the tides flowing in and out from the sea spins the turbines, which power an electrical **generator**.

Tides rise and fall everywhere in the world, twice a day, so tidal power is very reliable compared to other forms of renewable energy. Scientists might not be able to predict whether it will be sunny or windy, but they can predict the amount of electricity that tidal power systems will produce each day.

New York City in the **United States of America** has the world's first tidal turbines connected to a local electricity network. They are located in the East River, between Roosevelt Island and the borough of Queens.

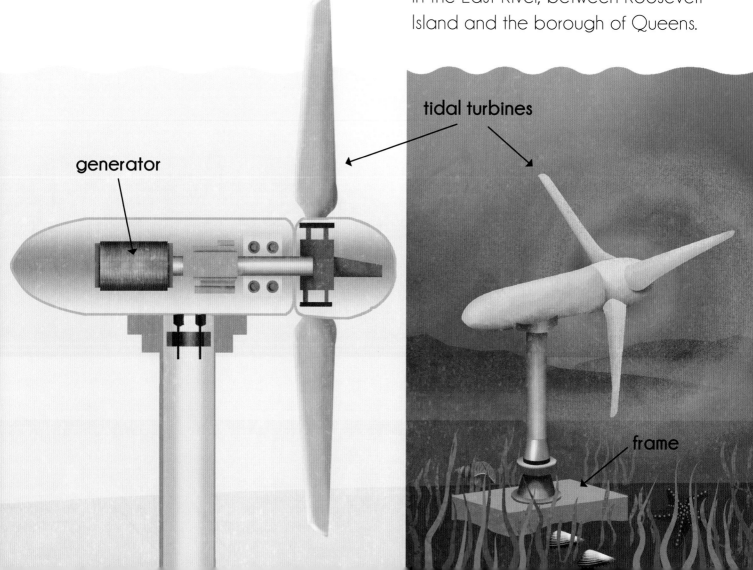

generator

tidal turbines

frame

Geothermal Power

The extreme heat from deep under Earth's surface can be used to make electricity. This is known as geothermal energy.

Scientists and engineers dig wells in areas where there is a lot of heat stored deep below the ground. They inject cold water into one well, where it is heated by the hot rocks. This creates steam. The steam and hot water are collected through a second well. The steam is then separated from the hot water in a **separator** and used to spin a **turbine**. The turbine is connected to

a **generator** to make electricity. The leftover hot water, which is not needed to spin the turbines, passes through a **cooling tower** before being pumped back underground.

In the green hills of **Kenya**'s Great Rift Valley in East Africa, you can find the Olkaria steam fields. Deep wells use rising steam from the ancient rocks to supply electricity for the surrounding area. The electricity is shared with people living in different areas by connecting electrical **transmission lines**.

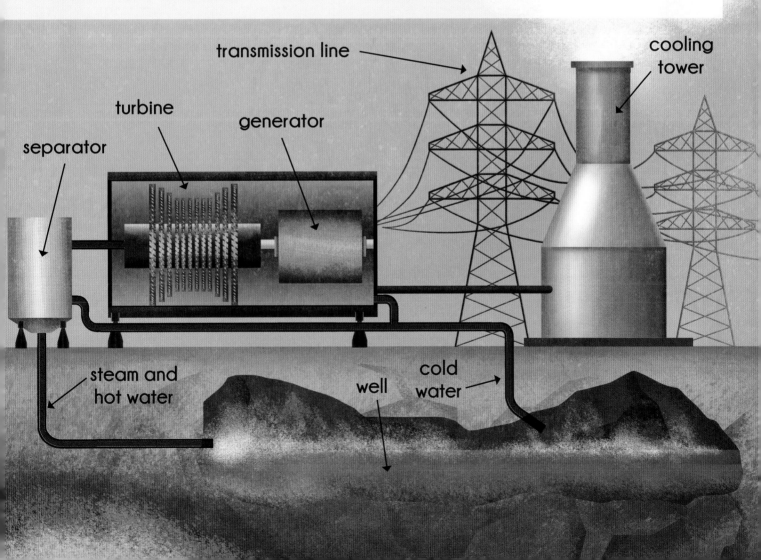

transmission line

cooling tower

turbine

generator

separator

steam and hot water

well

cold water

Wave Power

Just like a surfer uses waves to move a surfboard, the motion of waves can also be used to make electricity.

In **Gibraltar**, the British territory located at the southern tip of Spain, a new type of wave energy machine has been developed. **Buoys** float up and down on the surface of the water, causing liquid to move through a **motor**, which powers a **generator**.

Unlike some wave energy systems which are anchored to the sea floor far offshore, the buoys in Gibraltar are connected to buildings onshore. This makes them easier to reach for the scientists who keep them running and for the engineers who connect their power to the nearby electrical transmission lines.

The wave power in Gibraltar supplies local businesses with renewable electricity.

motor

generator

buoy

liquid tanks

Renewable Energy: The Way of the Future

With renewable energy projects now spreading around the world, change is coming. You can be part of this change with some easy steps to help protect the planet:

- Find out where your electricity comes from. Maybe your family or school could be buying renewable energy.

- Become an energy hero! Turn off the lights when you leave a room. Instead of turning up the heat in the winter, grab an extra layer of clothing to stay warm. These actions will help to save electricity for everyone who needs it.

- Most importantly, enjoy being curious about your world and encourage others to do the same!

For Dylan — from rhyming stories read at bedtime to exploring coastlines, bike trails and mountains, you remain the greatest adventure of my life — S. P. C.

To all those who never cease to be amazed by the vitality, strength and beauty of our planet — A. B.

Barefoot Books would like to thank **Dave Parkin**, Director, Progressive Energy and **Dr. Adam Wilson**, Professor of Geography, Environment & Sustainability, University at Buffalo for their help in the editing of this book.

Barefoot Books
23 Bradford Street, 2nd Floor
Concord, MA 01742

Barefoot Books
29/30 Fitzroy Square
London, W1T 6LQ

First published in United States of America
by Barefoot Books, Inc and in Great Britain
by Barefoot Books, Ltd in 2021
All rights reserved

Graphic design by Elizabeth Jayasekera, Barefoot Books
Edited and art directed by Emma Parkin, Barefoot Books
Reproduction by Bright Arts, Hong Kong
Printed in China on 100% acid-free paper
This book was typeset in Champagne & Limousines,
Eugene and Graphen
The illustrations were prepared using digital techniques

Hardback ISBN 978-1-64686-278-8
Paperback ISBN 978-1-64686-279-5
E-book ISBN 978-1-64686-343-3

British Cataloguing-in-Publication Data: a catalogue
record for this book is available from the British Library

Library of Congress Cataloging-in-Publication Data
is available under LCCN 2021933838

1 3 5 7 9 8 6 4 2

Barefoot Books
step inside a story

An environmental geologist, nature lover, educator and climate journalist, **Stacy P. Clark** enjoys distilling science into lively rhymes for young readers. Working between New York City and Dallas, Texas, she is inspired by the awesome potential of renewable energy to transform the way that countries around the world are powered. She loves exploring Central Park with her dog, Luna, and cycling along scenic trails and coastlines with her family.

Annalisa Beghelli is a freelance illustrator and also the founder of FA131, a company that advises on engaging in social responsibility through picture books. She graduated from Mimaster Illustrazione based in Milan where she currently lives and works. Annalisa has also illustrated *Home for a Penguin, Home for a Whale* for Barefoot Books.